BUGS

Termite

Kris Hirschmann

KIDHAVEN PRESS
An imprint of Thomson Gale, a part of The Thomson Corporation

THOMSON
— ✦ — ™
GALE

Detroit • New York • San Francisco • San Diego • New Haven, Conn. • Waterville, Maine • London • Munich

25.70

For more information, contact
KidHaven Press
27500 Drake Rd.
Farmington Hills, MI 48331-3535
Or you can visit our Internet site at http://www.gale.com

LIBRARY OF CONGRESS CATALOGING-IN-PUBLICATION DATA

Hirschmann, Kris, 1967
  Termite / by Kris Hirschmann.
    p. cm. — (Bugs)
  Includes bibliographical references (p.   ) and index.
  ISBN 0-7377-1776-9 (hardcover : alk. paper)
  1. Termites—Juvenile literature. I. Title. II. Series.
  QL529.H57 2005
  595.7'36—dc22
                                                        2005005124

Printed in The United States of America

CONTENTS

What Is a Termite?

The ermites are insects that have been infesting the earth for more than 100 million years. There are about 2,000 different types of termites. Most species live in warm areas, such as tropical rain forests and the hot, dry parts of Africa and Australia. But termites can be found in colder climates, too. These bugs are found as far north as Canada, France, China, and Japan. They also live in every

Opposite: In this magnified image of a dry-wood termite's head, the insect's mouthparts and antennae are visible.

5

extreme southern area except Antarctica and the lower tip of South America.

The Termite Body

Termites have no bones inside their bodies. Instead, they have outer coverings called **exoskeletons**. Most insects have hard exoskeletons, but termites do not. Their exoskeletons are flexible. Still, the termite's exoskeleton is tough enough to protect its tender inner parts. The exoskeleton is usually creamy white or yellowish in color.

Most termites are small. These insects usually measure between .25 inch and .5 inch (6mm to 12mm) when fully grown. King and queen termites, however, may be much larger. King termites often reach 1 inch (2.5cm) in length. In some species, the queen may measure 4 inches (10cm) from tip to tip.

The flexible exoskeleton of this South American termite is covered with thousands of tiny hairs.

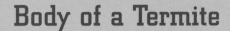
Body of a Termite

Two antennae can move in any direction. Tiny hairs on the antennae pick up touch and scent information.

The termite breathes through tiny holes in its thorax and abdomen.

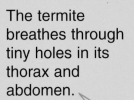

Six legs with special receptors sense vibrations.

A South African termite uses its claws and jointed legs to cling to a plant stem.

Three Parts

The termite body has three parts: the **head**, the **thorax**, and the **abdomen**. The rounded head is at the front of the body. It bears a mouth opening, mouthparts, and two short, straight **antennae.**

Behind the head is the thorax, which has three segments. A pair of jointed legs is attached to each segment. The six legs end in claws that let termites cling to rough surfaces, even when they are upside-down.

Next comes the abdomen, which is connected to the thorax by a thick waist. The abdomen is large and rounded, and it has ten segments. Most of the termite's internal organs are found inside the abdomen. The abdomen (as well as the thorax) is also lined with holes through which the termite breathes.

Termite Senses

Nearly all termites are blind. Most termites do not even have eyes. So instead of seeing the world, termites use their senses of touch, smell, hearing, and taste to make their way around.

The termite's most important senses are probably touch and smell. Scents are detected by two antennae. The antennae can also gather information by touching things or by being touched. A termite can swivel its antennae in any direction. As the antennae move, tiny hairs on these feelers pick up touch and scent information and send it to the termite's brain.

Hearing is also very important to termites. But termite hearing is not like human hearing. Instead of sensing sound vibrations in the air, termites pick up vibrations from things they touch. They detect these vibrations with special **receptors** on their legs.

Taste is the last sense on which termites depend. These bugs gather taste information with receptors on their mouthparts. Along with the other senses, taste gives a termite the information it needs to survive.

This magnified side view of a termite head shows its sensitive beaded antennae, which provide smell and touch information.

A Big Family

Termites are social insects, which means they live together in family groups. A group of termites is called a **colony**.

In any termite colony, members are divided among three **castes: reproductives, soldiers,** and **workers.** Members of different castes play different roles. Reproductives create new termites, soldiers protect the colony, and workers do day-to-day jobs.

Opposite: Termite colonies like this one are divided into three groups, each with a different job to do.

11

The Royal Pair

Every termite colony is built around its two most important members, the king and the queen. A colony has just one king and just one queen. These reproductives may live for ten to twenty years—much longer than members of other termite castes. They hide deep within the nest and are carefully guarded by the rest of the colony.

Worker termites gather around the swollen body of their queen, waiting to carry off the eggs she lays (inset) to nursery cells.

The king and queen are guarded because they play a very important role in the colony. The king's only job is to mate with the queen, and the queen's only job is to lay eggs. Up to 30,000 eggs per day pop out of the queen's grossly swollen abdomen.

After the eggs emerge, they are picked up by workers. The workers carry the eggs to special nursery cells. Then they carefully put the eggs down. Worker termites will take care of the eggs until they are ready to hatch.

A South African termite and nymph (inset) feed on spongelike fungus.

Development

When termite eggs hatch, immature termites called **nymphs** come out. The nymphs are tiny, but they look like miniature adults.

Nymphs grow through a process called **molting**. To molt, a nymph lies down and curls its body. This makes the exoskeleton crack along the back. The nymph then crawls out of the crack, leaving the old skeleton behind. The newly molted nymph is very soft at first. But its skin soon hardens into a new, larger shell.

Nymphs do not belong to any caste. They may develop into any kind of adult, depending on the needs of the colony. Each time a nymph molts, its body becomes more and more like its adult form. After many molts, a nymph reaches its adult size and shape.

Most nymphs develop into wingless soldiers or workers. A few, however, grow wings and reproductive organs and become dark in color. These termites are called **alates**. Their job is to leave the nest and create new colonies.

Swarming

When the time is right, worker termites make exit holes in the nest. Alates leave the nest through the holes and fly through the air in a huge **swarm**. Many are eaten by birds and other predators, but some survive and land.

Opposite: These reproductive termites known as alates have left their nest. Having shed their wings, they are ready to start a new colony.

The first nymphs in a new colony usually develop into soldiers, like this termite, and workers.

After landing, alates shed their wings. Females lift their abdomens and give off a scent that attracts males. They choose mates. Paired off, a male and a female walk together until they find a good nesting site. They dig a small nest and mate.

Very soon the new queen lays eggs. The queen and king take care of the first batch of eggs. Once the eggs hatch, the nymphs that emerge grow into soldiers and workers. These termites will take care of the king, the queen, and the brand-new colony.

Master Builders

Termites are the master builders of the insect world. Workers make huge nests in many different shapes and sizes. Once they are built, these nests are guarded by soldiers. With daily care and protection, a termite nest can last for dozens of years.

Subterranean Termites

Most termites live underground or have connections between their nests and the ground. These

Busy subterranean termites are at work protecting their underground home. Most termite species live underground.

species are called **subterranean termites**, and they are responsible for the most incredible termite nests on Earth.

In some parts of Africa and Asia, colonies of more than 1 million subterranean termites build mounds that tower 30 feet (9m) above the ground. The outer walls of the mounds are made of soil and are as hard as concrete. Inside, the mounds have many chambers. The lowest chambers reach far below the earth's surface.

In tropical rain forests, some subterranean termites use a mixture of wood, dung, and saliva to build nests high in trees. The main nest is big enough to hold thousands of termites. Workers also build tunnels from the nest to the ground so they can safely travel up and down the tree.

Not all termite nests are so easy to see. Different types

of subterranean termites may nest in tree trunks, mounds of soil, or other convenient places. The nests of these species do not have any distinct outward shape.

Dry-Wood Termites

Some types of termites never enter the soil. These termites are called **dry-wood termites**. Dry-wood species live inside pieces of wood, carving out chambers and tunnels to make a comfortable home.

Subterranean termites in Western Australia build enormous mounds, which tower over the flat landscape.

The dry-wood termite is extremely destructive and can live in any kind of wood, even inside furniture.

Sometimes these termites make openings to let alates leave the nest or to dump waste products outside. But they close up these openings as soon as they are done using them.

Dry-wood termites can live in any type of wood. They can be found in healthy trees or dead trees. They can even be found in furniture and the wooden supports inside the walls of people's homes. The termites cannot be seen from the outside—but they are doing great damage. Over time they eat away their wooden homes until nothing but a thin outer shell remains.

Climate Control

One of the main functions of a termite nest is climate control. Termites like warm, damp living conditions, and their nests help to create this environment.

The termite mounds of Africa and Asia are well known for this feature. These mounds act like natural chimneys. Hot, stale air leaves the nest from holes in the top of the mound. Cool, fresh air

This termite mound in Africa reaches the treetop with its chimneylike top. Termites open and close holes in the mound (inset) to control air flow.

enters from holes near ground level. Worker termites can open or close holes as needed to control the air flow.

It is amazing that insects can use such complicated building techniques. But this work comes naturally to termites. Wherever they live, these master builders always create the perfect homes.

CHAPTER

4

Staying Alive

Like all insects, termites spend their time just trying to stay alive. To do this, they must eat and avoid being eaten. Finding food is the job of the workers. Protecting the colony from **predators** is the job of the soldiers.

Finding Food

Most people think of termites as wood eaters. In reality, these insects will eat anything that contains

cellulose. Good termite foods include not only wood but also plant matter, paper, leather, wool, and fungi.

Most termites get food by **foraging**. Workers leave the nest at any time of the day. They look for food, leaving **scent trails** as they wander. Other termites follow these scent trails, and soon a long line of termites stretches from the nest. Eventually the termites find a food source. They gather seeds, grasses, and other materials and bring them back to the nest. Then they store the food until it is needed.

Instead of foraging, some termites grow their own fungus gardens. Special rooms inside the nest are used as growth chambers. Bits of fungus are removed from the gardens and eaten as necessary.

Dry-wood termites have yet another way of getting food. These termites eat as they make

A pair of termites comes across a leaf as they forage for food.

Opposite: Responsible for guarding the colony, the termite soldier uses its large pinchers for defending and attacking.

their homes bigger. They munch on the wooden walls around them and never leave their nests.

Eating Food

Only worker termites eat real food. They chew it well and then pass it through their bodies. In the gut, the food is broken down by countless one-celled **protozoa** that live inside the termite. It is changed into sugars that give the termite the energy it needs to survive.

When a nymph, soldier, or reproductive wants to feed, it approaches a worker. It begs by stroking the worker's body. In response, the worker gives off food-rich drops of liquid from its mouth or its abdomen. These drops are sucked down by the hungry beggar.

Termites as Prey

Termites are not just eaters. They are also eaten by many other animals. Common enemies include

Some termites grow their own fungus as food. Here, a South African termite nymph feeds in a fungus garden.

insects such as driver ants and larger animals such as aardvarks. These creatures sometimes attack termite nests, killing and eating as many termites as they can.

If a termite nest is attacked, an alarm message spreads quickly through the colony. Workers pick up eggs and carry them deeper into the nest, where they will be safer. At the same time, soldiers rush outward. They gather at the threatened spot and get ready to defend their home.

Soldier termites are well built for defense. Soldiers of all species have large heads that can block holes, and most have powerful pinchers. These sharp pinchers can kill attacking insects and hurt larger predators. One type of termite, the nasutus, has an extra weapon. Its head ends in a nozzle that sprays sticky poison. This poison kills some predators and scares others away.

After an attack, many colony members are dead, and the nest may be damaged. But many termites

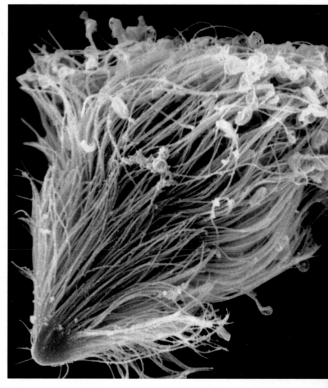

Tiny one-celled organisms called protozoa live in a termite's gut, helping it to digest food.

An ant overpowers and kills a termite soldier. Termites are food to many predators.

remain. The workers fix the nest while the soldiers keep a lookout. Very soon the nest is back to normal. With luck, the colony will survive for many termite generations yet to come.

GLOSSARY

abdomen: The rear segment of a termite's body.

alates: Reproductives that leave the nest and build new colonies elsewhere.

antennae: A pair of feelers on the termite's head, used for touching and smelling.

castes: Subgroups of a termite colony. Members of different castes look different and have different jobs.

cellulose: A material found in the cell walls of plants.

colony: A family group of termites.

dry-wood termites: Termites that never enter the soil but live only inside wood.

exoskeletons: Skeletons on the outside of the body.

foraging: Traveling outside the nest to look for food.

head: The front segment of a termite's body.

molting: Casting off an old exoskeleton. Termites must molt in order to grow.

nymphs: Young termites before they grow into adults.

predators: Any animals that hunt and eat other animals.

protozoa: Single-celled organisms that live inside the guts of termites.

receptors: Organs that detect sensory information and send it to the termite's brain.

reproductives: Termites that can mate and produce new termites.

scent trails: Invisible lines of scent left

behind by termites when they forage.

soldiers: Termites whose job is to protect the colony.

subterranean termites: Termites that live underground or have connections between their nests and the ground.

swarm: A large group of termites that leaves the nest to mate and form new colonies. Swarming termites are called alates.

thorax: The middle segment of a termite's body.

workers: Termites that do the day-to-day work of the colony. Workers' jobs include building and repairing the nest, finding food, and caring for eggs.

FOR FURTHER EXPLORATION

Books

Sara Swan Miller, *Ants, Bees, and Wasps of North America.* New York: Franklin Watts, 2003. Learn about the three other families of social insects. Discusses the similarities and differences between these insects, the environments in which they live, and how to watch them.

W. Wright Robinson, *How Insects Build Their Amazing Homes.* Woodbridge, CT: Blackbirch, 1999. Describes the ways wasps, termites, ants, and bees build their houses and nests.

Carole Telford and Rod Theodorou, *Through a Termite City.* Des Plaines, IL: Heinemann Interactive Library, 1998. Take an illustrated tour through the most incredible termite homes on Earth.

John Woodward, *What Lives Under the Carpet?* Hauppage, NY: Barron's, 2002. Discover some of the many insects, including termites, that live in human homes.

Web Sites

Alien Empire (www.pbs.org/wnet/nature/alienempire). This PBS Web site has a wealth of information about insect anatomy, behavior, homes, and more.

Just for Kids (www.terminix.com/Fun/Kids). Click on the links to play bug games, do bug activities, create your own bugs, and much more.

Termites (www.woodmagic.forprod.vt.edu/kids/Termite). This Web site is a good basic introduction to termites.

INDEX

PICTURE CREDITS

ABOUT THE AUTHOR

Kris Hirschmann has written more than 100 books for children. She is the president of The Wordshop, a business that provides a variety of writing and editorial services. She holds a bachelor's degree in psychology from Dartmouth College in Hanover, New Hampshire.

Hirschmann lives just outside Orlando, Florida, with her husband, Michael, and her daughters, Nikki and Erika.